The Diary

I Talk You Talk Press

CONTENTS

I Talk You Talk Press

CHAPTER ONE

Liam was walking home from work. It was 8:00pm, but it was summer, so the sky was still light. He had had a long day at the supermarket. He worked in the storeroom of the supermarket. He had to lift heavy boxes all day. He was looking forward to going home and having a bath.

He crossed the road. Then, he saw something on the pavement. It looked like a book. He picked it up. It had a brown leather cover.

It's a diary, he thought. *Someone has dropped their diary. Should I leave it here? Or should I look inside it? Maybe there is an address. I can take it to the person.*

He opened the diary and looked at the personal details page. There was a name and an address. The name was Richard Woking. The address was in Notting Hill. It was an address in a nice part of London. He looked at the schedule section. Richard seemed busy. There were appointments for many days.

Today is Thursday, he thought. Friday was empty, but on Saturday, there was an appointment. ---- *7:00pm North Café* ----

I should take it to Richard's house, thought Liam. *I'm tired, but Richard has an appointment on Saturday. If he doesn't have this diary, he might forget. Tomorrow night, I'm going out for drinks with my friends, so I can't take it tomorrow.*

Liam was tired, but he decided to take the diary to Richard's house. He walked back to the Underground station and took the train across London.

I've never been to Notting Hill before, he thought. *That area is too expensive for me.*

He got off the train at Notting Hill Gate, and went up the stairs. He went outside. The address was Pembridge Square. He looked on his phone. It was not so far from the train station.

I can walk, he thought. He walked down a street called Pembridge Gardens.

Wow, the houses are big, he thought. *I'm sure this person is rich.*

He walked to Pembridge Square and found the house. The house was tall. It had many floors.

Maybe this house has twenty rooms! he thought. *My apartment only has one room. This is like a different world!*

He opened the gate and walked up the steps. He rang the bell. There was a camera next to the bell.

"Hello?" said a woman's voice.

"Hello. I found Mr Woking's diary, so I came to return it," said Liam.

The woman was quiet.

"Hello?" said Liam. "Can you hear me?"

A few seconds later, the door opened.

CHAPTER TWO

Liam looked at the woman. She was about 50 years old, and she was wearing expensive designer clothes. She had short blonde hair. She looked rich.

"Sorry to bother you," said Liam. "I found this. Maybe it is your husband's?"

The woman took the diary and looked at it.

"It is not my husband's," she said. "We moved into here about two months ago. This diary belongs to the man who lived here before."

"Oh, really? Maybe he forgot to update his address in the diary. Do you have his new address? He has an appointment on Saturday."

"Pardon?" asked the woman.

"He has an appointment on Saturday."

The woman looked at Liam strangely.

"But that is impossible!" said the woman.

"Why?" asked Liam.

"Because Mr Woking died four months ago!"

Liam looked at the woman. "He...he died?"

"Yes. He was a famous writer."

"A famous writer? I don't know him," said Liam.

"Well, he wrote history books," said the woman. "They are not so popular. But people in universities read them. He was often on TV, talking about historical events. I can't remember the details...but...this diary. It is not Mr Woking's diary."

"So why is his name in the diary?" asked Liam.

"I don't know," said the woman. "Now it is August. He died in April. It can't be his diary."

She looked at the pages for January, February, and March.

"This is strange," she said. "There are not many appointments, but there are meetings at Oxford University, and history groups. So maybe this is Mr Woking's diary. But…where did you find it?"

"I found it in Hackney."

"Hackney? But Mr Woking would never go there! It's a dangerous place."

Liam smiled a little. "I live in Hackney," he said quietly.

"Oh! I'm sorry!" said the woman. "I didn't mean to say anything bad…"

"It's OK," said Liam.

The woman gave Liam the diary. "I'm sorry. I can't help you," she said.

"No problem," said Liam. "I'm sorry I bothered you. Have a nice night."

The woman smiled and closed the door. Liam walked down the steps and closed the gate.

This is strange. I have the diary of a famous man. A dead famous man! And the dead man has an appointment at seven pm in a café on Saturday!

CHAPTER THREE

When Liam got home, it was late. He heated a frozen pie in the microwave and ate it while watching TV. He was single, and lived alone. He had a girlfriend for four years, but they broke up last year. He was looking for a new girlfriend, but he hadn't found one. So, he spent most evenings at home, alone, watching TV, or surfing the Internet.

He ate his pie quickly, because he was hungry. He couldn't concentrate on the TV. He was thinking about the diary. It was on the sofa next to him. He opened it and looked at the schedule for January to April. The month of April was empty.

He died in April, thought Liam. He looked at May. There were no appointments. May was empty. Then, in June, July and August, there were appointments. He compared the style of writing. The writing style was beautiful. The writing from January to March was the same as the writing style from June to August.

How can Richard Woking write in his diary if he is dead? he thought. *Did he plan his schedule for the full year? Did he write his schedule for June to August before he died? But, why are April and May empty? And why was his diary on a road in Hackney? I need to find out more about Richard Woking.*

He picked up his smartphone and googled Richard Woking. There were many results. He clicked the first one. It was from the BBC. It was about Richard's death. Liam read it. Richard had been a famous writer of history books. He had often been on TV. He had taught at Oxford University. He had died at the beginning of April of a heart attack. He was 75 when he died.

5

So it is true, thought Liam. *The woman in Notting Hill was right. Richard was a famous history writer. And he is dead.*

He looked at the diary again. It was a mystery. Then, Liam had an idea. *The schedule for Saturday says 7:00pm North Café. Where is North Café?* He googled North Café. It was a small café in Camden. It looked like a café for young people. He looked at a picture of Richard Woking. Richard had white hair and a white beard. He didn't look like the type of person to go to North Café.

Maybe he planned to meet a young researcher there, thought Liam. Then he thought, *But he is dead!*

He put the diary and his smartphone on the sofa and opened a can of beer. Then, he had an idea.

I will go to North Café at seven o'clock on Saturday! Maybe I can solve the mystery!

CHAPTER FOUR

The next day, Liam worked hard in the supermarket. He didn't like his job. It was hard, and he didn't get much money. But he liked his co-workers. He liked one co-worker very much. Her name was Sandy. She worked on the cash register at the front of the shop. He wanted to be Sandy's boyfriend, but there was a problem. Sandy already had a boyfriend. Liam had been looking for a girlfriend for a while. He had tried online dating, but he hadn't met anyone he liked.

When he was at work, he worried about his life.

Will I be alone forever? he thought as he lifted heavy boxes. *Maybe I will find someone tonight.*

Every Friday night, Liam went to bars with his friends, Steve and Jason. Steve and Jason had girlfriends. When they went out, they always looked for a girlfriend for Liam, but they never found one. Liam was shy. It was difficult for him to talk to new people.

After work, Liam walked home, and had a shower. He heated a frozen pizza and some chips in his microwave and ate them quickly. He got changed. He was wearing smart grey jeans and a white T-shirt. He was looking forward to the night out with his friends, but he was also thinking about Saturday.

Who will I meet in North Café? he thought. *I will tell Steve and Jason about it. They will be very surprised.*

Thirty minutes later, Liam, Steve and Jason were sitting in a pub beer garden. It was still warm outside, and the cold beer tasted delicious. The pub beer garden was crowded and noisy.

"So, how was your week Liam?" asked Jason.

"Something really strange happened," said Liam.

"Strange? You got a girlfriend?" asked Steve. Jason and Steve laughed.

"No. That's not funny," said Liam. "Something really strange. I was walking home last night, when I found a diary on the ground. I picked it up. There was a name and address inside. It belonged to Richard Woking, and the address was Notting Hill."

"Notting Hill? That's an expensive area," said Steve.

"I know. And I found it near my apartment in Hackney. I thought it was strange," said Liam.

"So what did you do?" asked Steve.

"I looked in the diary. There were appointments for tomorrow and next week. So, I thought, If Richard doesn't have the diary, he will have trouble. So I took it to his house."

"That's kind of you," said Jason. "Was Richard pleased?"

Liam took a drink of his beer and smiled. "Well, a strange thing happened. A woman answered the door. I said, 'I found your husband's diary.' She looked at it and said, 'Richard Woking used to live here. He was a famous writer of history books. But he doesn't live here anymore. He died in April.'"

"What?" said Steve.

"If he's dead, how can he have appointments in his diary? And how can he drop his diary in Hackney?" asked Jason. Steve and Jason thought it was very strange.

"I don't know."

"So what did you do?" asked Steve.

"I went home and googled Richard Woking. It's true. He was a famous writer of history books. And he taught history at Oxford University sometimes. Sometimes he was on TV. He died in April."

Steve and Jason thought about it. "Do you think his ghost is walking around London?" asked Jason.

Steve and Liam laughed. "I don't think so," said Liam.

"So what are you going to do with the diary?" asked Steve.

"Well, there is an appointment for seven o'clock tomorrow night at a café in Camden. I'm going to go to the café."

"You are going to go to the café? Why?" asked Jason.

"I don't know," said Liam. "Maybe it will help me solve the mystery."

"I have an idea. Richard made a plan to meet someone in the café.

He wrote it in his diary. And then he died," said Steve.

"Yes, I think so too," said Jason.

"But it is strange. He died in April. Then in May, there were no appointments. May is empty in the diary. Then the appointments started again in June. Why are there no appointments in April and May?" asked Liam.

Jason and Steve thought about it. "Is the writing from January to March the same style as the writing from June to now?" asked Jason.

"Yes," said Liam. "It's the same."

"That's really strange," said Steve. "It's a ghost. Maybe you will meet a ghost tomorrow in the café!"

Jason laughed. "Liam doesn't need to meet a ghost. He needs to meet a nice girlfriend! Come on, let's go to the next bar. Maybe Liam will find a girlfriend there, and then he can take her to the café tomorrow!" The three men finished their drinks and walked out of the beer garden.

CHAPTER FIVE

Liam woke up at 10:00am the next morning. He drank a lot with Steve and Jason, and he had a headache. He got up and drank a lot of water.

What shall I do today? he thought. Then he remembered. *I'm going to the North Café tonight!*

He had a shower and made some egg on toast for breakfast. He was feeling nervous. *Who will I meet at the café tonight?* he thought. *Maybe I won't meet anyone there. Maybe Steve was right. Maybe Richard planned the meeting before he died. But I have no other plans for tonight. So I'll go.*

It was raining, so Liam spent the day at home. He surfed the Internet and watched TV. He also took a nap because he was tired. He had got home at 2:00am.

He made some curry for dinner and ate it around 5:00pm. Then, he got ready to go out. He dressed casually. There were pictures of the café on the Internet. It was a small café, and it looked casual. He left his apartment around 6:15pm. He carried the diary in a small bag.

If I leave now, I will get there a little early, he thought. He got the Underground train to Camden and walked to the café. It was in a small street, but he used the map on his phone to find it. He stood outside and looked at it.

Why would a famous man like Richard Woking come here? he thought. *This looks old and cheap. It looked better on the Internet.*

He opened the door, and went inside. It was dark inside the café. The walls were painted black. It looked old. There was a small counter and a few tables and chairs. A young couple were sitting at one of the tables. There was a man sitting at the counter. Liam sat down at a table in the corner. The waitress came over to him. He looked at the menu and ordered a coffee.

He looked at the time on his phone. It was 6:55. The young couple left the café.

Another five minutes, he thought. The waitress brought him a cup of coffee and he waited. And waited. At 7:15, he thought, *No one is coming. Maybe Steve was right. This was a bad idea.*

Then, the man at the bar started shouting. "Hey! Bring me another coffee!" he shouted the waitress.

That's so rude! thought Liam. *Did Richard Woking plan to meet this man? Why would he meet such a rude man?*

The man turned around and looked at Liam. Liam looked at the man.

"Are you looking at me?" asked the man angrily. "What do you want?"

"Er, sorry," said Liam. "Could I ask you a question?"

"What is it?" shouted the man.

"Are you waiting for a man called Richard Woking?" asked Liam.

"Who? A man? No! I'm not waiting for a man! Who are you? Why are you asking me that?"

The man seemed very angry, so Liam said, "I'm sorry. I made a mistake."

"Yeah, you made a mistake," said the man. He turned around again. "Hey! Where is my coffee? Why are you so slow?" he shouted to the waitress.

He is not a nice man, thought Liam. *I don't feel safe in here. I think I'll go.*
Liam paid for his coffee and walked out.

"Yeah! Get out!" shouted the man.

Wow! He is really angry! thought Liam.

Liam walked to the Underground train station. *What should I do about the diary?* he thought. *Maybe I should just forget about it. Should I throw it away? That seems bad. I'll think about it tomorrow.*

Liam got home about 45 minutes later. He watched TV, and then went to bed.

CHAPTER SIX

The next day, Liam woke up at 9:00am. He made some coffee, and thought about the diary while he drank it.

I shouldn't throw the diary away. It is a dead man's diary. But what can I do? Then, he had an idea. *Maybe Richard Woking has family! I could give it to his family!*

He picked up his computer, opened the Internet, and started to search. There was a lot of information about Richard Woking, but no information about his family. He thought about giving up, when he noticed something in the search results. It was a comment on a blog post about Richard. The comment said, ----*Richard was my grandfather. He was working on a book about the war when he died. Rebecca Woking.----*

Rebecca Woking! Maybe I can find her on Facebook! thought Liam. He opened up Facebook and started to search for Rebecca. Many names appeared.

There are many people called Rebecca Woking, he thought. *How will I know which one is Richard's granddaughter?*

He clicked on each profile and read the information. Some profiles had a lot of information made public, others were private. Then, he found one. The profile picture was of a woman with long brown hair. She looked around 30 years old. The cover photo showed the woman with an old man. They were holding a book. Liam looked closely at the book. The letters were small so he couldn't read them well, but he could see the word 'history'.

I think this is her! he thought. He looked for more information, but the account was private. *I'll send her a message.*

---- Dear Rebecca, I'm sorry to contact you so suddenly. But I was wondering, are you the granddaughter of Richard Woking? I found his diary a few days ago, and would like to return it to his family. Thank you. Liam Daniels.----

Liam pressed 'send'. *I hope she will see the message,* he thought. He spent the rest of the afternoon surfing the web.

In the evening, he made some pasta for dinner and ate it while watching TV. Then, his computer made a sound. He looked at it.

I got a message! he thought. He clicked on the Messenger icon on Facebook. There was a message from Rebecca.

-----Dear Liam, Richard Woking was my grandfather. Thank you so much for finding his diary and searching for me. I would like to have the diary back, and I would like to say 'thank you' in person. Would we be able to meet? Rebecca.---

Liam typed his reply.

----Dear Rebecca, I am so glad I found you. I finish work at 5:00pm on weekdays. Would one evening this week suit you? Liam.----

Rebecca replied.

----How about tomorrow night? Where is good for you?----

Liam thought about it. Then, he wrote,

----How about North Café in Camden? Your grandfather was planning to go there. How about 6:30pm?----

Rebecca replied.

----That's fine. See you then.----

Liam logged out of Facebook.

Maybe the mystery of the diary will be solved tomorrow! he thought.

CHAPTER SEVEN

The next day, Liam couldn't concentrate at work. The diary was in his bag in the staffroom. He would go directly from work to the North Café.

"What's wrong Liam? You have moved that box three times," said Mike, his co-worker.

"Oh, sorry. I just have something on my mind, that's all," said Liam.

"A girl?"

Liam smiled. "No, well, yes…well, kind of."

Mike laughed. "Are you in love?"

Liam shook his head. "No. I'm just meeting someone after work."

"A date?" asked Mike.

"No. I found something belonging to someone. I'm going to give it back."

"I see," said Mike. "But you like her, don't you?"

"I don't even know her!" said Liam.

Liam thought about it. *The picture on Facebook was nice. She's very pretty. But I don't know her. She probably has a boyfriend or is married.*

Liam tried to concentrate on his work for the rest of the day.

At 5:00pm, Liam and Mike were in the staffroom. They had finished work, and were getting ready to leave.

"So, what time is your date?" asked Mike.

"Six thirty. And it's not a date. I'm giving her something."

"What are you giving her?" asked Mike.

Liam took the diary out of his bag. "This," he said.

"What is it?"

Liam told Mike the story about the diary.

"Wow, that's a strange story," said Mike. "I'd like to hear what happens."

"I'll tell you tomorrow," said Liam. "See you then."

He put the diary back in his bag and walked out of the room.

He looked at the time. It was 5:15pm.

I will probably get there early, he thought. *But that's OK. It's better to be early than late.*

He walked out of the supermarket. It was a sunny evening. He walked to the Underground train station. It was a busy time. Many people were finishing work and going home. He went into the station and waited for the train.

I feel nervous, he thought. *Why do I feel nervous? Maybe because I'm going to solve the mystery of the diary.*

The train was packed. He was glad to get off. He walked up to street level and out into the warm air. He was thirty minutes early, so he spent some time walking around the local shops.

At 6:20, he went to the café. There were a few people inside – some tourists, a couple, and a man on his own.

Rebecca is not here yet, he thought. He sat down at a table. The waitress came over to him.

"I'm waiting for someone. I'll order when she arrives," he said.

"Sure," said the waitress. She walked away. Liam took the diary out of his bag and waited. He didn't have to wait long. A few minutes later, a woman came into the café. She looked around. Liam waved.

"Rebecca?" he said.

She looked over at him. "Liam?"

"Yes." Liam stood up. Rebecca walked over to him and they shook hands. They sat down and the waitress came over. They ordered two coffees.

"Well, here is your grandfather's diary," said Liam.

Rebecca held the diary and smiled. She looked like she was going to cry. Liam watched her.

Rebecca was wearing a blue summer dress and had her hair tied back.

She's beautiful, he thought. *And she seems so pleased to get her grandfather's diary. I'm sure she loved her grandfather very much.*

She looked at Liam. "This is so important to me," she said. "Thank you. Thank you."

Liam smiled. "Not at all," he said. The waitress brought the coffees over and went away. Rebecca looked at the back pages of the diary.

"Oh no!" she said. "The photograph!" She looked at Liam. "Did you see a photograph in here?" she asked.

"A photograph? No," he said.

Rebecca started to cry. "It was a photograph of my grandfather and I when I was a young girl. He kept it in his diary. It was a very special photograph to me and my grandfather."

"I'm so sorry," said Liam. "But I didn't find a photograph."

Rebecca was quiet for a few minutes. She wiped her eyes with a tissue.

"Could you tell me the story?" asked Liam. "I know your grandfather died in April. Why was his diary on the ground in a street in Hackney?"

Rebecca put the diary on the table and looked at Liam. "OK, I'll tell you the story," she said.

CHAPTER EIGHT

"My grandfather was a famous writer of history books. Sometimes, he was on TV. He also taught at Oxford University. But he always had time for me. When I was a child, he visited our house and played games with me for hours. I loved him very much. When I got older, he took me to his lectures. They were always very interesting. Because of him, I became interested in history. I thought about studying it at university, but I loved music too. So I chose music."

"What do you play?" asked Liam.

"I'm a singer," said Rebecca. "I trained to be an opera singer, but really, I like jazz. I want to be a jazz singer. But it is difficult. But my grandfather always supported me. When I performed in a concert with a jazz band in a club, he came to watch." Rebecca smiled. "Most of the people watching were young. But he didn't mind. He was proud of me. He said to everyone, 'That singer is my granddaughter.' Of course, I was proud of him too."

Rebecca stopped and took a drink of coffee.

"He was healthy. But one day at the beginning of April, he suddenly had a heart attack, and died. I was so upset." Rebecca was crying. "I cried for weeks. In May, my parents took everything out of his house. They decided to sell it. In his house, they found his diary. They gave it to me. I decided to use it. I felt closer to my grandfather. So, that is why you found the diary. I was using it."

"I see!" said Liam. "But, the writing in the diary from January to April is the same as the writing from June to August."

Rebecca smiled. "When I was a child, my grandfather played

games with me. He also taught me how to read and write. Of course, I learnt how to read and write at school, but my grandfather helped me. His handwriting was beautiful. When I was ten, I asked him to teach me how to write like him. I practiced for many hours, writing the alphabet in the same style. So, I write like my grandfather."

"I see," said Liam again. "Now I understand. But…I hope you don't mind me asking this…I found the diary in Hackney. It is a very different place from your grandfather's area of Notting Hill. Do you work in Hackney?"

"No. The day I dropped the diary, I was hurrying to a meeting with a club owner. I wanted to sing in his club, so I had sent him an email. He agreed to meet me to talk about it. He has an office in Hackney, so I was going to see him. But the train was late, and I was in a hurry. The diary fell out of my bag. It was a very bad day. I lost my grandfather's diary, and the club owner said 'no' to me."

"I'm sorry to hear that," said Liam.

"And then I forgot my appointments, because I didn't have my diary." Rebecca picked up her diary and looked at the page for the past week.

"That's it! I had a plan to meet someone here, at seven o'clock on Saturday night. I couldn't remember the day. I thought it was Sunday. I came here on Sunday, but the man wasn't here."

"A man? Did you plan to meet a man here on Saturday?"

"Yes. I'm single. I'm looking for a boyfriend. I met a man at a concert. We agreed to meet here on Saturday at seven."

"I think it was good you didn't meet him," said Liam.

"Why?" asked Rebecca.

"I looked in the diary. I saw the appointment for Saturday. I thought, If I go the café at seven, maybe I can solve the mystery of the diary. So I came here. I saw the man. He was not a nice man. He was rude to the waitress, and he was very angry. He shouted at me! He seemed violent."

"Oh, really? Well, I'm glad I didn't meet him!" said Rebecca.

"Maybe it was good that you lost your diary," said Liam. "Maybe your grandfather was looking after you."

Rebecca smiled. "Maybe. And maybe it was good because I met you. You are so kind. Thank you."

Liam smiled. "I didn't do anything special."

"Yes, you did. And I want to say thank you. Would you let me take you out to dinner one night?"

Liam was surprised. "Dinner? You don't have to do that. Really, I didn't do anything special."

"Please. I would like to. And I'd like to hear about your life. Tonight, we only talked about my life."

"My life isn't interesting."

Rebecca smiled. "I'm sure it is. My grandfather often said, 'All lives are interesting'. I have a concert next Sunday afternoon. Would you like to come to it? We can go out for dinner after the concert."

"I'd love to!" said Liam.

Rebecca and Liam smiled at each other.

I have a date! thought Liam. *I'm so glad I found that diary! But what about the photograph? I must try to find it.*

CHAPTER NINE

Liam walked home. It was still light, and it was a nice evening. He walked to the place he found the diary. *Maybe the photograph fell out here,* he thought. He searched the road and the sides of the road, but he couldn't see a photograph.

A few days have passed since I found the diary, he thought. *The photograph will not be here. I will check in my house.*

Liam went home and looked in his house. He looked around his living room. He looked under the sofa and the table. There was no photograph.

Where did I take the diary? I took it to Notting Hill. Maybe the photograph fell out when I took it there. Maybe it fell out on the train. Maybe it fell out when I walked to Richard Woking's old house.

He thought about Rebecca. She had cried when she couldn't find the photograph. The photograph was very important to her.

I feel bad, thought Liam. *Maybe I dropped the photograph. I should try to find it. Or maybe….*

Liam thought about his visit to Richard Woking's old house. The woman in the house had opened the diary and looked through it. *Maybe it fell out in her front porch,* he thought.

The next day, after he finished work, Liam took the train to Notting Hill. He walked to Richard Woking's old house. While he walked, he looked at the side of the pavements for the photograph. He didn't find it. He walked to Richard's old house and opened the gate. He walked up the path and knocked on the door.

A few seconds later, the door opened.

"Can I help you?"

Liam looked at the woman. It was the same woman he spoke to before about the diary.

"Yes. I'm sorry to bother you again. I came here a few days ago. I told you about Richard Woking's diary. Well, I found his granddaughter, and I gave her the diary. But she said, 'There was a photograph of me and my grandfather in the diary.' I looked in the diary, but I can't find the photograph. I thought, *Maybe it fell out of the diary when I came here*. So now, I'm looking for it."

"A photograph!" said the woman. "Yes! My cleaner found a photograph. She showed it to me. But it didn't mean anything to me. It was here in the porch, under the mat."

"You found it? That's great! Can I have it please? I will give it to Richard's granddaughter."

"I'm sorry," said the woman. "My cleaner took it. She threw it away."

"Oh no!" said Liam. "Do you still have the garbage?"

"I'm not sure," said the woman. "Let me check." She went inside and closed the door.

Liam waited outside. *I hope she has the photograph,* he thought.

A few minutes later, the woman came back.

"Is this the photograph?" she asked.

Liam looked at it. It was a photograph of a man with a young girl. The girl looked like Rebecca.

"Yes! This is the photograph!" said Liam. "But...but...it's dirty and ripped."

"Yes. My cleaner threw it away. It was in the garbage. I'm sorry, but it is in very bad condition."

"Can I have it?" asked Liam.

"Of course," said the woman.

"Thank you. And I'm sorry to trouble you again."

The woman smiled and closed the door.

Liam went home. He looked at the photograph. It was dirty and ripped. *I can't fix the photograph myself,* he thought. *But maybe a photograph shop can help me.* He looked on his phone and found a photograph and camera shop. It was open from 9:00am to 5:00pm Mondays to Saturdays. *I work from Monday to Friday, so I can take it on Saturday,* he thought. *The day before I meet Rebecca. I hope the photograph shop can help me.*

CHAPTER TEN

On Saturday, Liam walked into the photograph shop. He went to the desk.

"How can I help you?" asked the woman.

Liam took the photograph out of his bag. "Could you clean and repair this photograph?" he asked. The woman looked at it.

"Hmm…" she said. "It is dirty, but I can clean that. It is ripped quite badly, but I think I can help. I can photograph it and use Photoshop."

"How long will it take?" asked Liam.

"A few days," said the woman.

"I need it tomorrow. It's very important," said Liam. "If you can do it today, I will pay extra."

The woman looked at her computer. "We are not so busy today. So I think I can do it. Come back at 5:00pm."

"Thank you so much," said Liam. He walked out of the shop and went home.

At home, he tried to watch the football on TV, but he was nervous. He was nervous about the photograph, and he was nervous about his date with Rebecca the next day. He tried to concentrate on the football and surf the Internet. At 4:30, he left his apartment and went to the photograph shop.

"How is it?" he asked the woman.

The woman showed him the photograph.

"Oh wow!" said Liam. "It looks new!"

"Yes, it took a few hours, but I could clean and fix it," said the woman.

"I will pay extra," said Liam.

"No, it's OK. Just the regular price is fine," said the woman. Liam paid the woman.

"Thank you so much! The girl in the photograph is a woman now. She will be so pleased!"

CHAPTER ELEVEN

The next day, Liam put on a smart shirt and black jeans, and went to the concert. It was in a small club. It started at 5:00pm. It was Liam's first time to go to a jazz concert. He went to the bar and got a beer. Then, he found a table and sat down. The other tables were full. After a few minutes, Rebecca and the band came on stage. Rebecca was wearing a long black dress.

She looks beautiful, thought Liam. *And I have a date with her after the concert! I'm so lucky!*

The band began to play, and Rebecca started to sing.

Wow, she has a beautiful voice, he thought. Liam enjoyed the concert. It finished an hour later. The other people watching the concert got up and left the building. Liam stayed at his table and waited for Rebecca. After fifteen minutes, Rebecca came over to Liam's table. She had got changed, and was wearing jeans and a white shirt.

"Sorry to keep you waiting," she said. "Did you enjoy the concert?"

"It was great!" said Liam. "Your voice is amazing!"

Rebecca smiled. "Thank you. Do you like Indian food? There is a nice Indian restaurant just around the corner."

"I love Indian food," said Liam. "But before we go, I want to give you something."

"What is it?" asked Rebecca.

Liam took a package out of the plastic bag he was carrying. He gave it to Rebecca. "Open it," he said.

Rebecca took it and opened it. When she saw the photograph, she started to cry.

"You found it!" she said. "Where did you find it?"

"It was found in your grandfather's old house," said Liam. "I got it from the new owner."

Rebecca hugged Liam. "Thank you so much!" she said. "You really are the kindest man I have ever met!"

Liam smiled. "No, I'm not. I just wanted to make you happy," he said. "Come on, let's go and eat!"

Rebecca linked arms with Liam and they walked out of the concert hall together.

"I think my grandfather wanted me to meet you," said Rebecca.

Liam smiled again. "I hope so!" he said.

THANK YOU

Thank you for reading The Diary. (Word count: 6,117) We hope you enjoyed it.

There are quizzes about this book on our free study site I Talk You Talk Press EXTRA. http://italk-youtalk.com

If you would like to read more graded readers, please visit our website http://www.italkyoutalk.com

Other Level 3 graded readers include
A Dangerous Weekend
A Holiday to Remember
Akiko and Amy Part 1
Akiko and Amy Part 2
Akiko and Amy Part 3
Be My Valentine
Different Seas
Enjoy Your Business Trip
Enjoy Your Homestay
I Need a Friend
Old Jack's Ghost Stories from England (1)
Old Jack's Ghost Stories from England (2)
Old Jack's Ghost Stories from Ireland
Old Jack's Ghost Stories from Japan
Old Jack's Ghost Stories from Scotland

Old Jack's Ghost Stories from Wales
Party Time!
Stories for Christmas
The Curse
Together Again
Who is Holly?

ABOUT THE AUTHOR

I Talk You Talk Press is a Japan-based publisher of language textbooks, graded readers and language learning/teaching resources.

Our team is made up of highly experienced language teachers and translators, who have all studied at least one additional language to an advanced level.

This experience enables us to design our materials from the perspective of both the teacher and the learner. We consult with both teachers and language learners when designing our textbooks and graded readers, and test our materials extensively in the classroom before publication.

We are a fast-growing press, and currently publish graded readers for learners of English. We publish new graded readers monthly.

Made in the USA
Columbia, SC
12 June 2024

36463265R00021